50 Best Canadian Cheese Recipes

By: Kelly Johnson

Table of Contents

- Classic Poutine
- Maple Bacon Mac and Cheese
- Cheddar Cheese Bannock
- Tourtière with Cheese Crust
- Baked Brie with Maple Syrup and Pecans
- Smoked Gouda Scalloped Potatoes
- Cheese-Stuffed Bannock Tacos
- Canadian Cheddar and Ale Soup
- Montreal Bagel Breakfast Sandwiches
- Grilled Cheese with Apple and Aged Cheddar
- Lobster Mac and Cheese
- Cheesy Saskatoon Berry Galette
- Butter Tart Cheesecake
- Cheese Curds with Spicy Ketchup
- Maple Cheddar Scones
- Wild Mushroom and Brie Puff Pastry Bites
- Cheesy Cauliflower Bake

- Cheddar and Dill Biscuits
- Grilled Peameal Bacon and Cheese Sliders
- Potato and Cheese Perogies
- Cheesy Cornbread with Jalapeños
- Cheddar-Stuffed Meatloaf
- Canadian Three-Cheese Pizza
- Mac and Cheese Poutine
- Spinach and Ricotta Stuffed Shells
- Broccoli Cheddar Soup
- Cheese-Stuffed Chicken Breasts
- Cheddar Cheese and Chive Muffins
- Cheesy Bacon Potato Skins
- Maple Cheddar Grilled Corn
- Roasted Garlic and Cheese Mashed Potatoes
- Brie and Cranberry Crostini
- Canadian Cheddar Quiche
- Cheese and Herb Popovers
- Cheddar-Topped Tourtière Pie
- Bacon and Cheese Breakfast Casserole

- Cheddar Beer Bread

- Mac and Cheese Stuffed Peppers

- Smoked Salmon and Cream Cheese Pinwheels

- Brie-Stuffed French Toast

- Cheddar Grits with Maple Glazed Sausage

- Cheese and Onion Pie

- Mushroom and Cheese Tart

- Maple Apple and Cheddar Hand Pies

- Cheese-Stuffed Meatballs

- Grilled Zucchini and Cheese Skewers

- Montreal Smoked Meat and Cheese Sliders

- Rustic Cheese and Tomato Galette

- Baked Mac and Cheese Balls

- Cheddar and Maple Glazed Donuts

Classic Poutine

Ingredients:

- 4 cups French fries (fresh or frozen)
- 1 cup cheese curds
- 2 cups brown gravy (beef or chicken-based)

Instructions:

1. Cook the fries until golden and crispy.
2. Heat gravy until hot but not boiling.
3. Plate fries, top with cheese curds, and pour hot gravy over to melt the curds slightly.
4. Serve immediately.

Maple Bacon Mac and Cheese

Ingredients:

- 300g elbow macaroni
- 200g sharp cheddar, grated
- 100g mozzarella, grated
- 4 slices bacon, chopped and cooked
- 2 tbsp flour
- 2 tbsp butter
- 2 cups milk
- 2 tbsp maple syrup
- Salt, pepper, pinch of nutmeg

Instructions:

1. Cook pasta and set aside.
2. In a saucepan, melt butter, stir in flour and cook 1 minute.
3. Slowly whisk in milk, simmer until thickened.
4. Add cheese, maple syrup, and seasoning.
5. Stir in pasta and bacon.
6. Optional: transfer to a baking dish, top with more cheese, and bake at 375°F (190°C) for 15–20 minutes.

Cheddar Cheese Bannock

Ingredients:

- 2 cups all-purpose flour
- 1 tbsp baking powder
- ½ tsp salt
- 1 cup grated cheddar
- ¾ cup water or milk
- 2 tbsp vegetable oil or melted butter

Instructions:

1. Preheat oven to 400°F (200°C).
2. Mix dry ingredients, stir in cheese.
3. Add liquid and oil to form a soft dough.
4. Shape into a round disk or drop as small rounds onto a baking sheet.
5. Bake for 20–25 minutes until golden.

Tourtière with Cheese Crust

Ingredients (Filling):

- 500g ground pork
- 1 small onion, finely chopped
- 1 garlic clove, minced
- ½ tsp allspice, ½ tsp cinnamon
- Salt, pepper
- ¼ cup broth

Cheese Crust:

- 2 cups flour
- 150g cold butter, diced
- 1 cup grated cheddar
- 4–6 tbsp cold water

Instructions:

1. Make the crust: cut butter and cheese into flour, add water to form dough. Chill.
2. Cook pork with onion, garlic, spices, and broth until liquid is reduced.
3. Line a pie dish with crust, add filling, cover with top crust.
4. Bake at 375°F (190°C) for 45–50 minutes.

Baked Brie with Maple Syrup and Pecans

Ingredients:

- 1 wheel Brie
- 3 tbsp maple syrup
- ¼ cup chopped pecans
- Puff pastry (optional)

Instructions:

1. Preheat oven to 375°F (190°C).
2. Place Brie in a baking dish or wrap in puff pastry.
3. Drizzle with maple syrup and sprinkle with pecans.
4. Bake for 15–20 minutes until soft and gooey.
5. Serve with crackers or baguette slices.

Smoked Gouda Scalloped Potatoes

Ingredients:

- 4 medium potatoes, thinly sliced
- 2 cups grated smoked gouda
- 2 tbsp flour
- 2 tbsp butter
- 2 cups milk
- 1 garlic clove, minced
- Salt, pepper

Instructions:

1. Preheat oven to 375°F (190°C).
2. Make a roux with butter and flour, whisk in milk and garlic, cook until thickened.
3. Layer potatoes in a dish, pouring sauce and cheese between layers.
4. Top with remaining cheese and bake 45–55 minutes until golden and tender.

Cheese-Stuffed Bannock Tacos

Ingredients:

- Bannock dough (see Cheddar Cheese Bannock recipe)
- 1 cup shredded cheese
- Taco fillings: seasoned beef, lettuce, tomato, sour cream

Instructions:

1. Flatten bannock dough into rounds, stuff each with cheese, fold and seal.
2. Fry in oil until golden and puffed.
3. Let cool slightly, cut open and fill with taco ingredients.
4. Serve warm.

Canadian Cheddar and Ale Soup

Ingredients:

- 1 onion, chopped
- 2 cloves garlic, minced
- 2 tbsp butter
- 2 tbsp flour
- 1 cup ale or beer
- 2 cups chicken broth
- 1 cup cream or milk
- 2 cups sharp Canadian cheddar, grated
- Salt, pepper, mustard powder

Instructions:

1. Sauté onion and garlic in butter until soft.
2. Stir in flour, cook 1 minute.
3. Add ale, simmer 2–3 minutes.
4. Add broth and simmer 10 minutes.
5. Stir in cream and cheese until smooth.
6. Season to taste and serve with crusty bread.

Montreal Bagel Breakfast Sandwiches

Ingredients:

- 2 Montreal-style bagels
- 2 eggs
- 2 slices cheddar or Swiss cheese
- 2–4 slices of bacon or peameal
- Butter
- Optional: avocado, tomato, or greens

Instructions:

1. Toast bagels and butter lightly.
2. Fry eggs to preference; cook bacon or peameal until crispy.
3. Layer egg, cheese, and meat on the bagel.
4. Add optional toppings. Close sandwich and serve hot.

Grilled Cheese with Apple and Aged Cheddar

Ingredients:

- 4 slices of bread (sourdough or multigrain)
- 1 apple, thinly sliced (e.g., Granny Smith)
- 4 slices aged cheddar
- Butter

Instructions:

1. Butter one side of each bread slice.
2. Layer cheddar and apple slices between unbuttered sides.
3. Grill in a pan over medium heat until bread is golden and cheese melts.
4. Serve immediately.

Lobster Mac and Cheese

Ingredients:

- 300g elbow macaroni
- 200g lobster meat (cooked and chopped)
- 200g cheddar or Gruyère
- 2 tbsp butter
- 2 tbsp flour
- 2 cups milk
- Salt, pepper, paprika, lemon zest (optional)

Instructions:

1. Cook macaroni and set aside.
2. Make a roux with butter and flour, whisk in milk, and simmer until thick.
3. Stir in cheese, then lobster and pasta.
4. Optional: Transfer to baking dish, top with breadcrumbs and bake at 375°F (190°C) for 15 minutes.

Cheesy Saskatoon Berry Galette

Ingredients:

- 1 pie crust (store-bought or homemade)
- 1 cup Saskatoon berries (or blueberries)
- 1 tbsp cornstarch
- 1 tbsp sugar
- ½ tsp lemon zest
- ½ cup soft cheese (ricotta or mild goat cheese)

Instructions:

1. Preheat oven to 375°F (190°C).
2. Roll out dough. Spread soft cheese in the center, leaving a 2-inch edge.
3. Toss berries with sugar, cornstarch, and zest, then pour over cheese.
4. Fold edges over. Bake 30–35 minutes until golden and bubbling.

Butter Tart Cheesecake

Ingredients (Crust):

- 1½ cups graham cracker crumbs
- ¼ cup melted butter
- 2 tbsp brown sugar

Filling:

- 2 packs cream cheese (room temp)
- ½ cup brown sugar
- 2 eggs
- 1 tsp vanilla
- ½ cup raisins or pecans (optional)

Topping (Optional):

- ¼ cup maple syrup
- 1 tbsp butter
- ¼ cup chopped pecans

Instructions:

1. Preheat oven to 325°F (160°C).
2. Mix crust and press into a pan. Bake for 8 minutes.
3. Beat filling ingredients until smooth. Pour over crust.

4. Bake 35–40 minutes. Cool and chill.

5. Optional: Add maple pecan topping before serving.

Cheese Curds with Spicy Ketchup

Ingredients:

- 1 cup cheese curds
- ½ cup flour
- 1 egg, beaten
- ½ cup breadcrumbs
- Oil for frying

Spicy Ketchup:

- ½ cup ketchup
- 1 tsp hot sauce
- ½ tsp smoked paprika
- 1 tsp vinegar

Instructions:

1. Dredge curds in flour, egg, and breadcrumbs. Chill 15 min.
2. Fry until golden and crisp.
3. Mix spicy ketchup ingredients. Serve warm.

Maple Cheddar Scones

Ingredients:

- 2 cups flour
- 1 tbsp baking powder
- ½ tsp salt
- ½ cup cold butter
- 1 cup grated sharp cheddar
- ⅓ cup maple syrup
- ½ cup milk

Instructions:

1. Preheat oven to 400°F (200°C).
2. Combine dry ingredients, cut in butter, stir in cheddar.
3. Add maple syrup and milk to form a soft dough.
4. Pat into a circle and cut into wedges.
5. Bake 18–20 minutes until golden.

Wild Mushroom and Brie Puff Pastry Bites

Ingredients:

- 1 sheet puff pastry
- 1 cup wild mushrooms, chopped and sautéed
- 100g Brie, cubed
- 1 egg, beaten

Instructions:

1. Preheat oven to 375°F (190°C).
2. Cut puff pastry into squares.
3. Add mushrooms and a cube of Brie to center.
4. Fold corners slightly or leave open.
5. Brush with egg and bake for 15–18 minutes.

Cheesy Cauliflower Bake

Ingredients:

- 1 large head cauliflower, cut into florets
- 2 cups shredded cheddar cheese
- 1 cup heavy cream or milk
- 2 tbsp butter
- 2 tbsp flour
- 1 tsp mustard powder
- Salt and pepper to taste
- ½ cup breadcrumbs (optional)

Instructions:

1. Preheat oven to 375°F (190°C).
2. Steam or boil cauliflower until just tender. Drain well.
3. In a saucepan, melt butter, whisk in flour, and cook 1 minute.
4. Slowly add cream, whisking until thickened. Stir in cheese and mustard powder until melted. Season with salt and pepper.
5. Place cauliflower in a baking dish, pour cheese sauce over it. Sprinkle breadcrumbs on top if using.
6. Bake for 20–25 minutes until bubbly and golden.

Cheddar and Dill Biscuits

Ingredients:

- 2 cups all-purpose flour
- 1 tbsp baking powder
- ½ tsp baking soda
- ½ tsp salt
- 6 tbsp cold butter, diced
- 1 cup shredded sharp cheddar
- 2 tbsp fresh dill, chopped
- 1 cup buttermilk

Instructions:

1. Preheat oven to 425°F (220°C).
2. Mix dry ingredients, cut in butter until crumbly.
3. Stir in cheddar and dill.
4. Add buttermilk and mix gently to form dough.
5. Pat dough onto a baking sheet and cut into rounds or squares.
6. Bake 12–15 minutes until golden.

Grilled Peameal Bacon and Cheese Sliders

Ingredients:

- 12 slider buns
- 12 slices peameal bacon
- 12 slices cheddar or Swiss cheese
- Butter
- Mustard or mayo (optional)

Instructions:

1. Grill peameal bacon until cooked and slightly crispy.
2. Butter slider buns and toast on grill.
3. Assemble sliders with bacon, cheese, and condiments.
4. Place sliders back on grill or in oven briefly to melt cheese. Serve warm.

Potato and Cheese Perogies

Ingredients:

- 2 cups mashed potatoes
- 1 cup shredded cheddar cheese
- 2 cups all-purpose flour
- 1 egg
- ½ cup sour cream
- ½ cup water
- 1 tsp salt

Instructions:

1. Mix flour, egg, sour cream, water, and salt to make dough. Knead and roll thin.
2. Combine mashed potatoes and cheese.
3. Cut dough into circles, fill with potato-cheese mix, fold and seal edges.
4. Boil perogies until they float, then optionally pan-fry until golden.

Cheesy Cornbread with Jalapeños

Ingredients:

- 1 cup cornmeal
- 1 cup all-purpose flour
- ¼ cup sugar
- 1 tbsp baking powder
- ½ tsp salt
- 1 cup milk
- 1/3 cup vegetable oil
- 2 eggs
- 1 cup shredded cheddar
- 1–2 jalapeños, diced (seeds removed for less heat)

Instructions:

1. Preheat oven to 400°F (200°C).
2. Mix dry ingredients.
3. In a separate bowl, whisk milk, oil, and eggs.
4. Combine wet and dry ingredients, fold in cheese and jalapeños.
5. Pour into greased baking pan, bake 20–25 minutes.

Cheddar-Stuffed Meatloaf

Ingredients:

- 1 lb ground beef
- 1 lb ground pork
- 1 cup breadcrumbs
- 1 egg
- 1 small onion, finely chopped
- 2 cloves garlic, minced
- 1 cup shredded cheddar cheese
- ½ cup milk
- Salt and pepper

Instructions:

1. Preheat oven to 350°F (175°C).
2. Mix beef, pork, breadcrumbs, egg, onion, garlic, milk, salt, and pepper.
3. Form half of the mixture into a loaf shape on a baking sheet.
4. Place cheese in a line down the center, cover with remaining meat mixture and seal.
5. Bake for 1 hour or until cooked through.

Canadian Three-Cheese Pizza

Ingredients:

- Pizza dough (store-bought or homemade)
- ½ cup pizza sauce
- 1 cup shredded mozzarella
- ½ cup shredded cheddar
- ½ cup crumbled goat cheese or feta
- Optional toppings: bacon, mushrooms, onions

Instructions:

1. Preheat oven to 475°F (245°C).
2. Roll out dough on pizza stone or baking sheet.
3. Spread sauce evenly, sprinkle cheeses and toppings.
4. Bake 12–15 minutes until crust is golden and cheese bubbly.

Mac and Cheese Poutine

Ingredients:

- 4 cups French fries
- 2 cups prepared mac and cheese (use your favorite recipe)
- 1 cup cheese curds
- 2 cups hot gravy

Instructions:

1. Cook fries until crispy.
2. Plate fries, spoon mac and cheese over them.
3. Add cheese curds on top and pour hot gravy over to melt.
4. Serve immediately.

Spinach and Ricotta Stuffed Shells

Ingredients:

- 20 jumbo pasta shells
- 1 cup ricotta cheese
- 1 cup cooked spinach, drained and chopped
- 1 cup shredded mozzarella
- ½ cup grated Parmesan
- 1 egg
- 2 cups marinara sauce
- Salt and pepper to taste

Instructions:

1. Preheat oven to 375°F (190°C).
2. Cook shells according to package, drain and cool.
3. Mix ricotta, spinach, mozzarella, Parmesan, egg, salt, and pepper.
4. Stuff each shell with mixture, place in a baking dish with half the sauce.
5. Top with remaining sauce and extra cheese.
6. Bake 25–30 minutes until bubbly.

Broccoli Cheddar Soup

Ingredients:

- 4 cups broccoli florets
- 1 cup shredded cheddar cheese
- 2 tbsp butter
- 1 onion, chopped
- 2 cloves garlic, minced
- 3 cups chicken or vegetable broth
- 1 cup milk or cream
- 3 tbsp flour
- Salt and pepper

Instructions:

1. Sauté onion and garlic in butter until soft.
2. Stir in flour and cook 1 minute.
3. Gradually whisk in broth and milk, simmer until thickened.
4. Add broccoli and cook until tender.
5. Blend half the soup for creaminess.
6. Stir in cheddar cheese until melted. Season and serve.

Cheese-Stuffed Chicken Breasts

Ingredients:

- 4 boneless chicken breasts
- 1 cup shredded mozzarella or cheddar
- ½ cup spinach, cooked and chopped
- Salt, pepper, and herbs
- Olive oil

Instructions:

1. Preheat oven to 375°F (190°C).
2. Cut a pocket in each chicken breast.
3. Mix cheese and spinach, stuff into pockets.
4. Season chicken, sear in oil 2-3 minutes per side.
5. Transfer to oven and bake 20–25 minutes until cooked through.

Cheddar Cheese and Chive Muffins

Ingredients:

- 2 cups flour
- 1 tbsp baking powder
- ½ tsp salt
- 1 cup shredded cheddar
- 2 tbsp chopped fresh chives
- 1 cup milk
- 1 egg
- ¼ cup vegetable oil

Instructions:

1. Preheat oven to 400°F (200°C).
2. Mix dry ingredients, stir in cheese and chives.
3. Combine wet ingredients, then mix with dry until just combined.
4. Spoon into muffin tin.
5. Bake 18–20 minutes until golden.

Cheesy Bacon Potato Skins

Ingredients:

- 4 large baking potatoes
- 1 cup shredded cheddar
- 6 slices bacon, cooked and crumbled
- ½ cup sour cream
- 2 green onions, chopped
- Salt and pepper

Instructions:

1. Bake potatoes until tender. Cool slightly, then cut in half and scoop out most of the flesh.
2. Mix potato flesh with cheese, bacon, salt, and pepper.
3. Spoon mixture back into skins.
4. Bake at 400°F (200°C) for 15 minutes until cheese melts.
5. Serve with sour cream and green onions.

Maple Cheddar Grilled Corn

Ingredients:

- 4 ears of corn, husked
- ½ cup shredded sharp cheddar
- 2 tbsp maple syrup
- 2 tbsp butter, melted
- Salt and pepper

Instructions:

1. Preheat grill to medium-high.
2. Brush corn with butter and grill, turning, until charred and tender.
3. Brush with maple syrup, sprinkle with cheddar, and let cheese melt slightly.
4. Season with salt and pepper. Serve warm.

Roasted Garlic and Cheese Mashed Potatoes

Ingredients:

- 4 large potatoes, peeled and cubed
- 1 head garlic
- 1 cup shredded cheddar
- ½ cup milk or cream
- 3 tbsp butter
- Salt and pepper

Instructions:

1. Preheat oven to 400°F (200°C). Slice top off garlic head, drizzle with oil, wrap in foil, and roast 30–40 minutes until soft.
2. Boil potatoes until tender.
3. Mash potatoes with roasted garlic cloves, butter, milk, and cheese.
4. Season and serve warm.

Brie and Cranberry Crostini

Ingredients:

- 1 baguette, sliced
- 200g Brie cheese, sliced
- ½ cup cranberry sauce
- Fresh thyme (optional)

Instructions:

1. Toast baguette slices until crisp.
2. Top each slice with Brie and cranberry sauce.
3. Warm under broiler until Brie softens slightly.
4. Garnish with thyme and serve.

Canadian Cheddar Quiche

Ingredients:

- 1 pie crust (pre-made or homemade)
- 1 cup shredded sharp cheddar cheese
- 4 eggs
- 1 cup heavy cream or half-and-half
- ½ cup cooked bacon, chopped
- ¼ cup chopped green onions
- Salt and pepper

Instructions:

1. Preheat oven to 375°F (190°C).
2. Place pie crust in a quiche or pie pan.
3. Spread bacon, cheese, and green onions evenly on crust.
4. Whisk eggs, cream, salt, and pepper, then pour over filling.
5. Bake 35–40 minutes until set and golden. Let cool before slicing.

Cheese and Herb Popovers

Ingredients:

- 1 cup all-purpose flour
- 1 cup milk
- 3 eggs
- 1 cup shredded cheese (cheddar, gruyère, or your choice)
- 2 tbsp chopped fresh herbs (parsley, chives, thyme)
- ½ tsp salt
- Butter for greasing

Instructions:

1. Preheat oven to 425°F (220°C).
2. Whisk flour, milk, eggs, and salt until smooth.
3. Fold in cheese and herbs.
4. Butter a popover pan or muffin tin, fill each about ¾ full.
5. Bake 20 minutes, then reduce heat to 350°F (175°C) and bake 15 more minutes until puffed and golden.

Cheddar-Topped Tourtière Pie

Ingredients:

- 1 lb ground pork (or mix pork and beef)
- 1 small onion, finely chopped
- 1 clove garlic, minced
- ½ tsp cinnamon
- ½ tsp cloves
- ¼ tsp nutmeg
- Salt and pepper
- 1 pie crust (bottom and top)
- 1 cup shredded cheddar cheese

Instructions:

1. Preheat oven to 375°F (190°C).
2. Cook pork, onion, and garlic until browned. Add spices, salt, and pepper. Let cool.
3. Line pie dish with crust, add meat filling.
4. Cover with top crust, seal edges, cut slits for steam.
5. Sprinkle cheddar on top crust.
6. Bake 45–50 minutes until crust is golden and cheese melted.

Bacon and Cheese Breakfast Casserole

Ingredients:

- 6 slices bread, cubed
- 8 eggs
- 2 cups shredded cheddar cheese
- 1 cup milk
- 6 slices cooked bacon, crumbled
- 1 small onion, chopped
- Salt and pepper

Instructions:

1. Preheat oven to 350°F (175°C).
2. In a greased baking dish, layer bread cubes, bacon, onion, and cheese.
3. Whisk eggs, milk, salt, and pepper, pour over casserole.
4. Let sit 15 minutes, then bake 45–50 minutes until set.

Cheddar Beer Bread

Ingredients:

- 3 cups self-rising flour
- 1 cup shredded cheddar cheese
- 1 bottle (12 oz) beer
- 2 tbsp sugar
- 2 tbsp melted butter

Instructions:

1. Preheat oven to 375°F (190°C).
2. Mix flour, cheese, and sugar.
3. Stir in beer until just combined.
4. Pour into greased loaf pan, drizzle butter on top.
5. Bake 45–50 minutes until golden and cooked through.

Mac and Cheese Stuffed Peppers

Ingredients:

- 4 large bell peppers, tops cut off and seeds removed
- 2 cups cooked macaroni and cheese
- ½ cup shredded cheddar
- ¼ cup breadcrumbs

Instructions:

1. Preheat oven to 375°F (190°C).
2. Stuff peppers with mac and cheese mixture.
3. Top with cheddar and breadcrumbs.
4. Place in baking dish with a little water at bottom.
5. Bake 25–30 minutes until peppers are tender and topping golden.

Smoked Salmon and Cream Cheese Pinwheels

Ingredients:

- 1 sheet puff pastry, thawed
- 4 oz cream cheese, softened
- 4 oz smoked salmon
- 1 tbsp chopped dill
- Lemon zest (optional)

Instructions:

1. Preheat oven to 400°F (200°C).
2. Spread cream cheese evenly over puff pastry.
3. Layer smoked salmon, sprinkle dill and lemon zest.
4. Roll pastry tightly, slice into ½-inch rounds.
5. Place on baking sheet and bake 12–15 minutes until golden.

Brie-Stuffed French Toast

Ingredients:

- 8 slices thick bread
- 8 oz Brie cheese, sliced
- 4 eggs
- 1 cup milk
- 1 tsp vanilla extract
- Butter for cooking
- Maple syrup to serve

Instructions:

1. Make sandwiches with Brie between two slices of bread.
2. Whisk eggs, milk, and vanilla.
3. Dip sandwiches in egg mixture, coat both sides.
4. Cook on buttered skillet over medium heat until golden and Brie melted.
5. Serve with maple syrup.

Cheddar Grits with Maple Glazed Sausage

Ingredients:

- 1 cup stone-ground grits
- 4 cups water
- 1 cup shredded sharp cheddar cheese
- 1 cup milk
- Salt and pepper
- 8 breakfast sausages
- ¼ cup maple syrup

Instructions:

1. Bring water to boil, slowly whisk in grits. Reduce heat and simmer 20–25 minutes, stirring often.
2. Stir in milk, cheese, salt, and pepper. Keep warm.
3. In a skillet, cook sausages until browned and cooked through.
4. Brush sausages with maple syrup and cook 1–2 minutes more to glaze.
5. Serve sausages over creamy cheddar grits.

Cheese and Onion Pie

Ingredients:

- 1 pie crust
- 2 cups shredded mature cheddar cheese
- 2 large onions, thinly sliced
- 2 tbsp butter
- 3 eggs
- 1 cup cream or milk
- Salt and pepper

Instructions:

1. Preheat oven to 375°F (190°C).
2. Sauté onions in butter until caramelized. Cool slightly.
3. Beat eggs with cream, salt, and pepper.
4. Spread onions and cheese in pie crust.
5. Pour egg mixture over filling.
6. Bake 35–40 minutes until set and golden.

Mushroom and Cheese Tart

Ingredients:

- 1 sheet puff pastry
- 2 cups mixed mushrooms, sliced
- 1 cup shredded Gruyère or Swiss cheese
- 1 small onion, diced
- 2 cloves garlic, minced
- 2 tbsp olive oil
- Salt, pepper, fresh thyme

Instructions:

1. Preheat oven to 400°F (200°C).
2. Sauté onion and garlic in olive oil until soft. Add mushrooms, thyme, salt, and pepper, cook until tender. Cool.
3. Roll out puff pastry on a baking sheet. Score a border around edges.
4. Spread mushroom mixture inside border, sprinkle cheese on top.
5. Bake 20–25 minutes until pastry golden and cheese melted.

Maple Apple and Cheddar Hand Pies

Ingredients:

- 2 sheets pie dough or puff pastry
- 2 apples, peeled, cored, and diced
- 1 cup shredded sharp cheddar
- 2 tbsp maple syrup
- 1 tbsp lemon juice
- 1 tsp cinnamon
- 1 egg, beaten (for egg wash)

Instructions:

1. Preheat oven to 375°F (190°C).
2. Toss apples with maple syrup, lemon juice, and cinnamon.
3. Roll out dough, cut into 4-6 circles.
4. Place apple mixture and cheddar on half of each circle, fold over and seal edges with a fork.
5. Brush with egg wash.
6. Bake 20–25 minutes until golden and puffed.

Cheese-Stuffed Meatballs

Ingredients:

- 1 lb ground beef or mixed meat
- 1 cup breadcrumbs
- 1 egg
- 2 cloves garlic, minced
- ½ cup grated Parmesan or shredded mozzarella
- Salt, pepper, herbs (parsley or oregano)
- 4 oz cheese cubes (mozzarella or cheddar)

Instructions:

1. Preheat oven to 400°F (200°C).
2. Mix meat, breadcrumbs, egg, garlic, Parmesan, salt, pepper, and herbs.
3. Take a handful of mixture, flatten, place cheese cube in center, and shape into meatball sealing cheese inside.
4. Place meatballs on baking sheet.
5. Bake 20–25 minutes until cooked through and golden.

Grilled Zucchini and Cheese Skewers

Ingredients:

- 2 medium zucchinis, sliced lengthwise into thin strips
- 8 oz halloumi or firm cheese, cut into cubes
- 2 tbsp olive oil
- 1 tbsp lemon juice
- Salt and pepper
- Fresh herbs (thyme, oregano)
- Wooden skewers (soaked in water)

Instructions:

1. Preheat grill to medium-high.
2. Toss zucchini strips with olive oil, lemon juice, salt, pepper, and herbs.
3. Thread zucchini strips and cheese cubes alternately onto skewers.
4. Grill 3–4 minutes per side until zucchini is tender and cheese has grill marks.
5. Serve warm.

Montreal Smoked Meat and Cheese Sliders

Ingredients:

- Slider buns
- 1 lb Montreal smoked meat, sliced thin
- 4 oz Swiss or cheddar cheese, sliced
- Mustard and pickles for serving
- Butter for toasting buns

Instructions:

1. Preheat skillet over medium heat.
2. Butter slider buns and toast until golden.
3. Layer smoked meat and cheese on bottom buns.
4. Heat in skillet covered until cheese melts.
5. Add mustard and pickles, top with bun. Serve immediately.

Rustic Cheese and Tomato Galette

Ingredients:

- 1 pie crust or puff pastry
- 2 large ripe tomatoes, sliced
- 1½ cups shredded cheese (Gruyère, mozzarella, or cheddar)
- 1 tbsp olive oil
- Salt, pepper, dried herbs (basil, oregano)
- 1 egg, beaten (for egg wash)

Instructions:

1. Preheat oven to 400°F (200°C).
2. Roll out crust on a baking sheet.
3. Spread cheese in center leaving a 2-inch border.
4. Arrange tomato slices on top of cheese, season with salt, pepper, and herbs.
5. Fold edges over tomatoes, brush crust with egg wash.
6. Drizzle olive oil over tomatoes.
7. Bake 30–35 minutes until crust is golden and cheese bubbly.

Baked Mac and Cheese Balls

Ingredients:

- 2 cups cooked macaroni and cheese (chilled)
- 1 cup breadcrumbs
- 1 egg, beaten
- Oil for baking or frying
- Optional: extra shredded cheese for filling

Instructions:

1. Preheat oven to 375°F (190°C).
2. Form chilled mac and cheese into small balls, optionally stuffing with extra cheese inside.
3. Dip balls into egg, then coat with breadcrumbs.
4. Place on baking sheet lined with parchment.
5. Bake 20–25 minutes until golden and crisp. (Or deep fry for extra crispiness.)
6. Serve warm.

Cheddar and Maple Glazed Donuts

Ingredients:

- 2 cups all-purpose flour
- ½ cup sugar
- 2 tsp baking powder
- ½ tsp salt
- ¾ cup milk
- 2 eggs
- 2 tbsp melted butter
- 1 cup shredded sharp cheddar
- Maple glaze: ½ cup maple syrup, 1 tbsp butter, pinch of salt

Instructions:

1. Preheat oil for frying to 350°F (175°C) or preheat donut maker.
2. In a bowl, mix flour, sugar, baking powder, and salt.
3. Whisk milk, eggs, and butter in another bowl. Combine wet and dry ingredients, fold in cheddar.
4. Pipe or spoon batter into donut molds or drop by spoonfuls into hot oil.
5. Fry or bake until golden and cooked through.
6. Warm maple syrup with butter and salt for glaze. Dip warm donuts in glaze. Serve.